D1491781

IMMEDIATE MEDIA^{CO}

First published in Great Britain in 2014 by Immediate Media Company London Limited, Vineyard House, 44 Brook Green, London W6 7BT

ISBN 978-0-9929364-1-9

© 2014 Immediate Media Company London Limited

All rights reserved. No part of this publication may be reproduced or transmitted in any form or by any means, electronic or mechanical, including photocopying, recording or any information storage and retrieval system, without prior permission in writing from the publisher.

The book is sold subject to the condition that it shall not, by way of trade or otherwise, be lent, resold, hired out or otherwise circulated without the publisher's prior consent in any form of binding or cover other than that in which it is published and without a similar condition including this condition being imposed on the subsequent purchaser.

Editor and design Shem Law
Copy editor Ron Hewit
Forewords Ben Preston & Paul Atterbury
Don Smith interview Andrew Duncan
Picture captions Researched and written by Patrick Mulkern, Ron Hewit & Shem Law
Picture research Roger Dixon & Tristan Hopkins
Designer Stuart Manning
Photography Simon Vinall & Derek Hillier
Thanks to Mark Braxton & Gill Crawford
Senior production co-ordinator Steve Calver
Image restoration and reprographic work Robert James, Martin McCormack & Ian Crabb
Project manager Jessica Batten

Printed and bound in the UK by Polestar Wheatons, Exeter

For *Radio Times*
Managing director, *Radio Times* **Group** Kathy Day
Associate Publisher Richard Campbell
Editor Ben Preston
Executive editor Tom Loxley
Radio Times Head of Heritage Ralph Montagu
Radio Times Head of Production Sharon Thompson

To order more copies of this book and other *Radio Times* products visit **radiotimes.com/ shoparchive** or call **0844 848 9739**

Love *Radio Times*? You can get a subscription here: **radiotimes.com/ magazinesubscription**

We welcome your feedback at *Radio Times* so please let us know what you think of this book: **feedback@radiotimes.com**

radiotimes.com

PLEASE NOTE

The *Radio Times* Archive is a working picture library. It has been much used (and abused) over the past 90 years. Many of the older prints and newer transparencies have no record of the photographer's name or the date the picture was taken. We have tried to identify, credit and contact photographers where we have the information and records to do so. Unfortunately that has not been possible in all instances. So if you are a photographer, or relative of a photographer, that we have not credited, please accept our apologies, and do please contact us at **feedback@radiotimes.com**

RadioTimes

FROM THE ARCHIVE

CLASSIC PHOTOGRAPHS FROM
THE PICTURE LIBRARY

DESIGNED & EDITED BY SHEM LAW

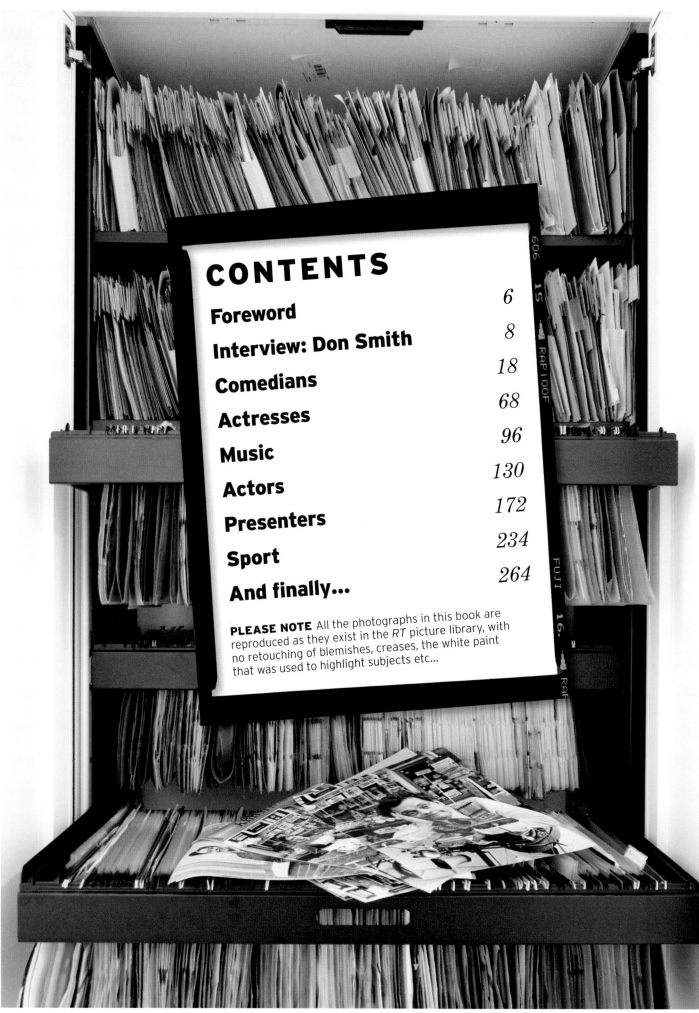

CONTENTS

PLEASE NOTE All the photographs in this book are reproduced as they exist in the *RT* picture library, with no retouching of blemishes, creases, the white paint that was used to highlight subjects etc...

The Radio Times Picture Library *Photograph by Ruth Roxanne Board 2014*

FOREWORD Down the back stairs, hidden between floors behind a nondescript door lies the *Radio Times* photo archive. A dark, dusty room and many cabinets bursting with hundreds of thousands of prints, negatives and transparencies.

This doesn't seem like a place to linger.

But pick any photograph from a pile and suddenly that changes. The hours melt away. Here, in a single room, is the story of Britain and broadcasting told through faces famous, familiar or half-forgotten.

There's Delia Smith, fag in mouth, serving a young Jamie Oliver in a grubby café. A cherubic John Betjeman staring skyward from beneath a trilby. Or Pan's People dancing bizarrely in silver boots, swathed in chains and what look like Christmas baubles.

Today, *Radio Times* is Britain's bestselling quality magazine, just as it has been since its launch in 1923. For the first three decades, in the days of radio, artists like Eric Fraser, Victor Reinganum and Edward Ardizzone held sway.

But with the advent of television, photography came to the pages of *Radio Times*. It allowed millions of readers to see another side to the polished stars beamed into their living rooms: Sammy Davis Jr smoking backstage (there really was a lot of smoking in the 60s); Jeremy Paxman actually looking relaxed; Jimmy Hill joshing with footballers in Coventry City's changing rooms.

Photography is good at immediacy and urgency. Yet what's striking about so many of the images in this book is their sheer ambition. An artfully created student bedroom (shades of Tracey Emin) marks Chris Evans's arrival on Channel 4's *Big Breakfast* in 1992. But for me the best pictures work because of their simplicity: David Attenborough by Nadav Kander is shot terrifyingly close in black and white; Tony Hancock is cold-ridden with a damp towel framing his face.

With the most talented people of their generation for subjects, it's no surprise that *Radio Times* has always attracted the most celebrated and accomplished photographers, including Don Smith, *RT's* staff photographer for more than 40 years, whose story you will find on page 8.

For too long their work appeared on our pages only to then lie hidden for years, literally, under the stairs. It's a delight to give these photographs the wider audience they deserve.

Ben Preston *editor, Radio Times*

Paul Atterbury
*Photographed at the Victoria & Albert Museum
by Sylvaine Poitau 2000*

PAUL ATTERBURY WRITES... A feature of any magazine office during much of the 20th century were the ubiquitous piles of photographs – in boxes, on shelves and in teetering towers of folders on the floor; blink and you'd trip. Supplied by photographers, writers, agencies or even readers, these prints and transparencies had all had their moment. Some had been published, some not, but once that moment had passed, they were discarded, as out of date as the issue of the magazine for which they'd been supplied. In more orderly magazines these photographs were eventually archived and turned into an informal photo library. In less organised places they were just dumped.

Happily, *Radio Times* followed the archive route and the collection of photographs they have carefully curated serves to remind us of the significance of radio and television in all our lives. Not just that, but with the passage of time these photographs also often acquire historical relevance.

The photographs included in this book, selected from the thousands filed away in the *Radio Times* office, offer an extraordinary, exciting, nostalgic, poignant and sometimes moving memory of the people brought to us by radio and television from the 1940s to the noughties. Some enjoyed a flickering kind of fame, many others remain in the spotlight, but all are part of the history of our time.

Photography is about two things: the subject and the photographer. In an ephemeral world, some photographers are quickly forgotten, yet their work lives on – often striking or even brilliant – despite being sadly now anonymous. This applies to these *Radio Times* images, but it is also the nature of photography, with many photographers, both amateur and professional, of the Victorian and later periods remaining firmly unknown despite the magnificence of their images. This is why, as a kind of social historian, I'm fascinated by photography. Since the 1840s, it has told us much about who we are and the world we live in. It easily endures and so it remains the most exciting and most accessible record of our history.

Today, in a digital age, none of this applies. Magazines no longer casually keep piles of old photographs, and ephemerality is guaranteed. Digital photography is universal but it does not endure. We all take thousands, millions of photographs, most of which will never be seen again. In 30 years' time, it's unlikely that anyone will be able to produce a second volume of this book, so make the most of what is a remarkable collection.

Paul Atterbury is a regular contributor to *Antiques Roadshow*

Harry H Corbett & Wilfrid Brambell
*Photographed on the set of Steptoe and Son
by Don Smith* 1970

Don Smith is the first, and only, *Radio Times* staff photographer, a job he fell into almost by accident, managing to survive ten editors, usually happily, sometimes not, all with different ideas. At 82, he still rides one of his ten bicycles 15 miles a day, plays bass in a jazz band and surveys his career with childish wonder verging on naivety and a total lack of arrogance.

"Photography led me to places and events, whether I enjoyed them or not, agreed with them or not, which were always enormously interesting. It was a very privileged position. Great fun, but not glamorous. I sometimes sat around for hours wondering if I'd get a decent picture."

Don Smith
Photograph
by Simon Vinall
2014

T HERE'S A PLETHORA of stories tumbling from him, always with the modest admonishment, "I don't want to boast or namedrop, but…" He tells of the time he photographed the then Kenneth Clark (subsequently Lord Clark) in France during filming of the 1969 BBC2 series *Civilisation*. "I didn't go abroad much and when I did I felt out on a limb, responsible for something I wasn't terribly sure about. Put me in a studio and I'm fine. Anyway, we started off in the Dordogne – sounds romantic but it wasn't – and although I got on well with him, I felt uneasy. He had enormous knowledge, and I had none.

"We ended up in Paris on 13 May 1968, the day the student riots started. If you didn't run fast enough, you got clubbed by the police. I thought how ironic to be working on a programme called *Civilisation*. People asked if I took a picture in the streets and I said, 'Not likely.' I didn't want to be beaten up.

"A photoshoot had been arranged of Clark standing with Notre Dame in the background. It was my big moment – I had a minute or so to do it. The tripod was set up, and he posed. Just as I had the shot nicely framed, he took out a cigarette. He was a heavy smoker. But in those days there were rules for *RT* covers – you couldn't show people drinking, smoking or in bed. How could I tell him he mustn't smoke? If he became moody, I wouldn't have a picture. What the hell should I do? I asked him to lower his right hand, a little more please, just a bit more, until the cigarette was practically hidden, and the picture was used.

"About a year later a book of the series was published. ▷

Kenneth Clark
*Photographed in Paris
by Don Smith* 1968

7 Paris RT2163 12·12·1961

RT2163-5

RT2163-19

RT2163-18

Frank Windsor

RT2163-27

James Ellis

Br

Jeremy

◁ I had to buy my own copy, but met him at the launch party. I assumed he wouldn't remember me, but he did and said he'd just given an address to the Royal Photographic Society where he was asked if photography was art and how much should be the work of the sitter and how much the photographer. He said 60/40 and added that in his experience only one person had the right balance – me. Maybe he said that to every photographer in the world.

"Sometimes I didn't know who I was photographing or why. I had to fish for answers in the nicest possible way, chatting to them – 'What do you do? That's interesting. How long have you done it?' It happened when I took a picture of Anthony Blunt [the Surveyor of the Queen's Pictures who was later unmasked as a Soviet spy]. Didn't have a clue who he was."

DON WAS BROUGHT up in Barnet, north London, the son of an engineer, and an interest in photography was instilled early. "I come from a family of skilled craftsmen who developed and printed their own pictures in an alcove under the stairs. My brother Peter, who was five years older than me, trained to be a cine photographer and seemed to have an exciting and interesting life, which I wanted to emulate. Sadly, he was killed doing National Service in 1947, but I started photography and have never done anything else."

He left school at 15 and became an industrial photographer, before being called up into the RAF where he continued taking pictures. After National Service he freelanced, and was then hired by Mirrorpic, an agency owned by the *Daily Mirror*. They had a contract with the BBC, which didn't in ▷

Z Cars contact strips
*Photographed on location
by Don Smith* 1961, 1967

Tony Hancock
Photographed on the set of Hancock's Half-Hour by Don Smith 1959

Alastair Sim
*Photographed at BBC Television Centre
by Don Smith* 1972

◁ those days have sophisticated still photographic equipment, and he was employed more or less full time with *Radio Times*. "Sounds weird, but it worked," he says. He was paid £15 a week, almost double his previous salary. "It wasn't bad for a 23-year-old."

His work was annotated meticulously in exercise books kept for him by "a wonderful lady called Hazel Jones who is now in her late 80s, and we're still in touch". They show how much film he used on a particular shoot, and that the first day he worked for *RT* was 4 November 1955 when, in the morning, he photographed a chart in the BBC newsroom showing where various foreign correspondents were in the world, and in the afternoon a singing group called the Stargazers who were in the BBC Showband.

"A few days later I photographed the actors Mai Zetterling and Robert Beatty for a play called *Idiot's Delight*. In those days most pictures were taken in rehearsal rooms, which were usually grotty church halls. It was terrible for me because they'd say the scene was supposed to be in a luxury flat overlooking Manhattan. You'd think, 'God, how can I make it look like that?' I usually used a blank wall as a backdrop." ▷

HE STAYED WITH MIRRORPIC for 12 years, through a couple of management changes before, he explains, "I became fed up with the way it was going, but we'll gloss over that. Meanwhile, the BBC was expanding and I applied for a job in the news department. I think I was going to be offered it, so I told *Radio Times* and they asked me to join the staff. My last assignment for the *Mirror* was on 30 March 1967 when I photographed the 20th episode of *The Forsyte Saga*. I did the concluding six episodes because I knew what was going on and the *Radio Times* staff, bless them, didn't.

"Sometimes they'd know what was happening in a particular series and sometimes I'd be told by the producer or director that, for instance, there was a story on *Z Cars* concerning Jimmy Ellis coming up in a few weeks. I had a knack of summing up the main feature of each episode and making damned sure I got what I thought was the right picture. In the early years it was very hit and miss and I took pictures that turned up years later as a cover.

"Once, in 1959, I was waiting in Ealing Film Studios to photograph Julie Andrews and wandered to another studio where a man was sitting down who I recognised as Ed Murrow – a very famous American war reporter. I asked if I could take his picture, did quite a nice portrait and two months later it was on the cover. Another time I saw Alastair Sim walking out of TV Centre and realised he must have been there for a reason, so I asked, 'Would you allow me to take a picture?' and he said, 'Of course, young man.' Again – on the cover months later.

"I insisted on doing my own developing and printing and had a dark room in the office at 35 Marylebone High Street. In those days the circulation was so vast – the Christmas issue sold nine million – so the only chance you had of pictures looking good was for the original to be pin sharp with good contrast."

Most subjects were cooperative – "we all wanted to do well" – but he remembers with some distaste Field Marshal Montgomery. "I don't like saying this because everyone has their good and bad days, but he was one person I came away with hatred. I went to his home, the Old Mill, in Alton, Hampshire, where they were recording an hour-long Christmas Day programme. He was terribly abrupt. After the first picture, he said, 'That's enough.' I replied, 'Hang on, I need a few more.' There were no electronic flashes in those days, just bulbs that burnt your fingers when you replaced them. I had to be quick, burnt myself, but took a couple more before he bundled me out into the very cold day.

"I walked down the path and saw an injured budgerigar. I knew he bred them, so I cuddled the bird next to my chest, went back, knocked on his door and said, 'Terribly sorry to bother you but I found this.' He shouted, 'It's not mine. Get out!' and pushed me down the steps. I put the bird in the footwell of my car and drove to Alton police station. They directed me to a terraced house where a chap bred them. He said, 'Poor little thing. Leave him with me and I'll nurse him back to health.' The comparison between those two men! Guess which one I held in the higher esteem.

MY WORKING DAYS were a great mixture – sometimes in a studio, or on a film location for a few days. Television was developing at a hell of a pace. In 1968, over a period of a few months I went to Malta to work on a series called *Vendetta*, then the Olympic Games in Mexico City to photograph the various stadiums. In those days there were currency restrictions. I was very raw and inexperienced, and *Radio Times* thought they were doing me a favour by booking me into the Hilton Hotel, which took up all my money. I didn't have a credit card.

"I wasn't at all well because of the city's altitude so luckily I didn't want to eat anything. If I'm honest it was an indifferent set of pictures because there's not much you can do with buildings. When I came back, I photographed the GB athletes in black and white. They're easy to get on with – no temperaments like some people and they weren't surrounded by PRs as they are today.

"I can't believe the amount of work I got through. It was a seven-day-a-week job and often long hours. My divorce [in 1978] was partially caused by that." He has a son, Peter, who works in Savile Row, and two grandchildren. "On one occasion I finished working at the Trade Union Conference in Brighton at 11 at night, drove home to north London and had to photograph the Duke of Rutland at Belvoir Castle at nine in the ▷

Ed Murrow
Photographed at Ealing Studios by Don Smith
1959

Field Marshal Bernard Law Montgomery, 1st Viscount Montgomery of Alamein
Photographed at his home in Hampshire by Don Smith 1961

How it all began...
Don Smith's work notebook showing his first assignments for Radio Times, starting on Friday 4 November 1955

Emma, Sophie with their father Eric Thompson
Photographed at Gairloch in the Highlands, with Florence and Dougal from The Magic Roundabout by Don Smith 1972

◁ morning. I drove there in my Humber estate – I needed a biggish car for all the equipment – and later that day did a job at the local radio station, and back in time to photograph an episode of *Porridge*. It was tiring and a hell of a responsibility.

"On certain jobs, where I knew I wouldn't get a second chance I took two cameras in case one messed up. I don't think I failed to bring back something usable, although it may not have been the best picture in the world."

In those days photography was mainly a working-class profession, but now it's been taken over by "artistes", with consequent rises in fees and, dare one say it, pretension. It's gone the same way as hairdressing, I suggest, a two bob cut turned into a 30 quid blow dry. "Yes, that's right. It's so different nowadays. I don't think I could do it. Cover photos

are elaborate set-ups, in studios, with hair and make-up specialists. I didn't know if my picture would be on the cover or not. I admire enormously the skills of today's photographers, but they're image-makers. If the picture isn't sharp, they can alter it and clean up the background. Mine were formed at the time. Today it can be done afterwards. It's technicians, not photographers, who have control. I sometimes ask if one or two photos make up a particular *RT* cover and they laugh at me because it could be five. Knowing what a complex magazine *RT* is to produce I have total admiration."

As relaxation he used to be a competitive cyclist. When he stopped working he decided to ride ten miles every day, doubling it the following year. "The actual mileage isn't difficult, but finding time is – two and a half hours – so I went

16

home, checked the undamaged bike he'd been riding – "I could walk by then and wondered if I'd get on the saddle. I did, but didn't know if I'd be able to balance, so I went on the pavement, and rode 13 and a half miles that day, and every other day since. I'm not boasting. It's simple if you're fit to start with."

He's taken over a million pictures, but doesn't have a favourite. "You might get a very good one out of a bad situation, which is better than one where everything went your way. Several years ago I had a telephone call from the Midlands from a man who ran the Tony Hancock appreciation society. He said that according to their records I'd photographed Hancock for six *Radio Times* covers. I'd never realised that. Towards the end of his life he was drinking heavily, but I never had any trouble and got on well with him. You have to know how far you can go and when to lay off. It can be irritating when photographers ask for 'just one more'. You don't want to bore your subject to death. I've never been very creative but I think I did shine in seizing the moment – which is difficult at times.

"I got on well with Harry H Corbett and Wilfrid Brambell in *Steptoe and Son,* although I believe they ended up hating each other. I photographed them hundreds of times, for every episode. I'd try for something that sums them up and noticed once they had a gilt picture frame on set. I asked Wilfrid to pose in it – nothing to do with the programme – but it worked."

Another time, the *Doctor Who* Appreciation Society wanted him to visit and identify various episodes. "I'd photographed them for years, but he knew more about it than I did. He identified one picture I took on 22 October 1966 for a cover on the Daleks for which I had no recollection."

ON OTHER OCCASIONS there were pleasant and unexpected surprises. "In the 70s I was told to get an overnight train to Glasgow, pick up a ferry, and photograph Eric Thompson, who narrated *The Magic Roundabout.* I had an aluminium case in which I put the figures of Dougal and Florence and I duly photographed him with on the edge of a loch. Then two little girls appeared – aged about ten and six – his daughters. I took a few pictures of them together and returned to London.

"Many years later in 1988 I was working in TV Centre on *The Winslow Boy*, which starred Gordon Jackson, who was great friends with Phyllida Law [Thompson's widow]. We were talking about Eric, who died very young [aged 53 in 1982], and Gordon said, 'Emma would love to know about that. She's starring in this as well.' I said, 'Emma who?' I'd never heard of her at that time, so I found the original negatives, did three sets of prints and gave one each to Sophie, Phyllida and Emma, who burst into tears."

As a semi-professional sideline he's played bass for many years with Mike Daniels and his Delta Jazzmen. "Last September we were at Tom Stoppard's bi-annual party at the Physic Garden in Chelsea and of course I'd photographed most of the guests, like Judi Dench, who were surprised to see me there. I'm aware, though, how few people I photographed are still alive."

He retired in 1992, but kept working for some years after. "I don't know how I survived all those editors – probably by producing usable pictures. Purely on the off chance sometimes. Hit and miss." Mostly hits? He chuckles. "I had my share."

Interviewer Andrew Duncan joined *RT* in 1990

back to ten. Last year I cycled 4,289 miles. I write down the distance every day, which is quite easy because once round my three local parks is 5.45 miles."

This year was less fortunate. He left his home at 8.45am on 14 January, didn't notice some black ice, slid and fell heavily, breaking his thigh and hip and injuring his pelvis. "What followed was a sitcom. An old man lying in the mud and slush, people coming to help, and I'm yelling, 'Don't go on the ice.' They head straight for it and fall over themselves."

He was taken to hospital and asked by seven doctors what daily medication he took. "None," he replied. No one believed him so surgery was postponed to the following day while his GP was contacted. He was in hospital for nine days and discharged to live with his son. A month later he returned

Hugh Laurie *Photograph by Jason Bell 2003*

COMEDY

(MEN +
WOMEN)

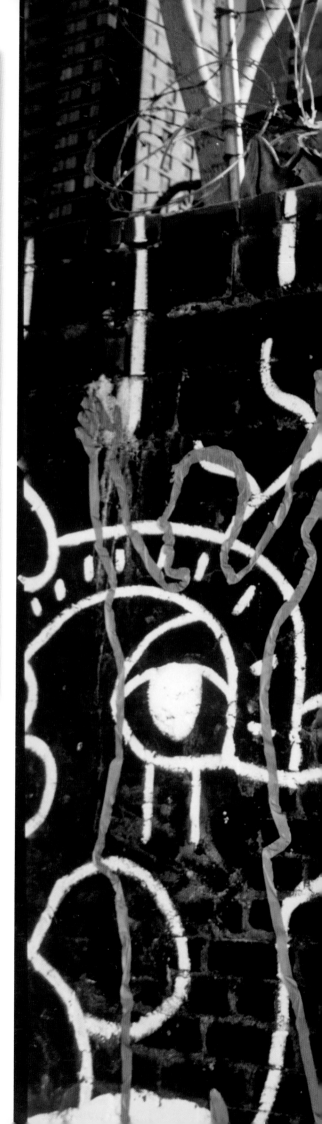

Peter Cook
Photograph by Don Smith 1971

Eddie Izzard
Photographed in New York by Jason Bell 2003

Ken Dodd with the Bluebell Girls *Photographer unknown. Blackpool* 1966

Ronnie Corbett
*Photograph by
Roger Jones* 1970

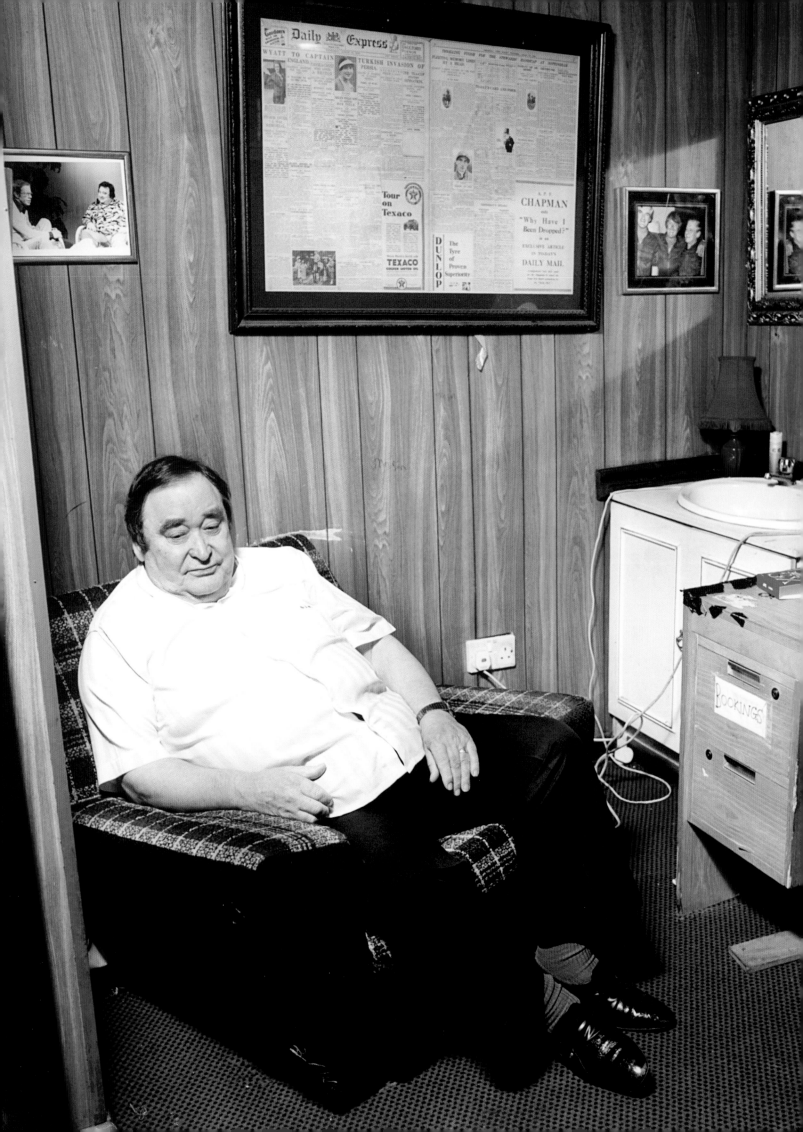

Jim Davidson
Photographed in Great Yarmouth by Mike Lawn 2003

Bernard Manning
*Photographed at his Embassy nightclub
in Manchester by Harry Borden 2002*

Sue Perkins & Mel Giedroyc
Photograph by Barry J Holmes 1999

Arthur Smith *Photograph by Mark Harrison 2002*

George Formby
Photographed on an ENSA (Entertainments National Service Association) tour of British troops in northern France. Photographer unknown March 1940

Marty Feldman *Photograph by Don Smith* 1973

Ben Elton
Photograph by Nigel Parry 1993

Terry Gilliam
Photographer unknown

Vic Reeves & Bob Mortimer
Photograph by Colin Bell 2004

Tony Hancock *Photograph by Don Smith* 1961

Tony Hancock *Photographed for Hancock's Half-Hour "The Cold" by Don Smith* 1960

Rob Brydon *Photograph by Colin Bell* 2004

Paul Whitehouse *Photograph by Trevor Ray Hart* 2003

NO SMOKING

Dressing Rooms

CARBON DIOXIDE
FIRE EXTINGUISHER
TEL 01706 655712

Joan Rivers
Photographed in the scenery dock at
BBC Television Centre by Jason Bell 2004

Arthur Askey *Photograph by Don Smith* 1974

Aimi MacDonald, Peter Jones, Nicholas Parsons, Kenneth Williams & Clement Freud *Photographed for the 100th edition of Just a Minute by Don Smith* 1971

Kenneth Williams *Photographs by Ray Rathborne* late 1960s

Leonard Rossiter *Photograph by Tony Ray-Jones*

Denis Norden *Photograph by Don Smith* 1972

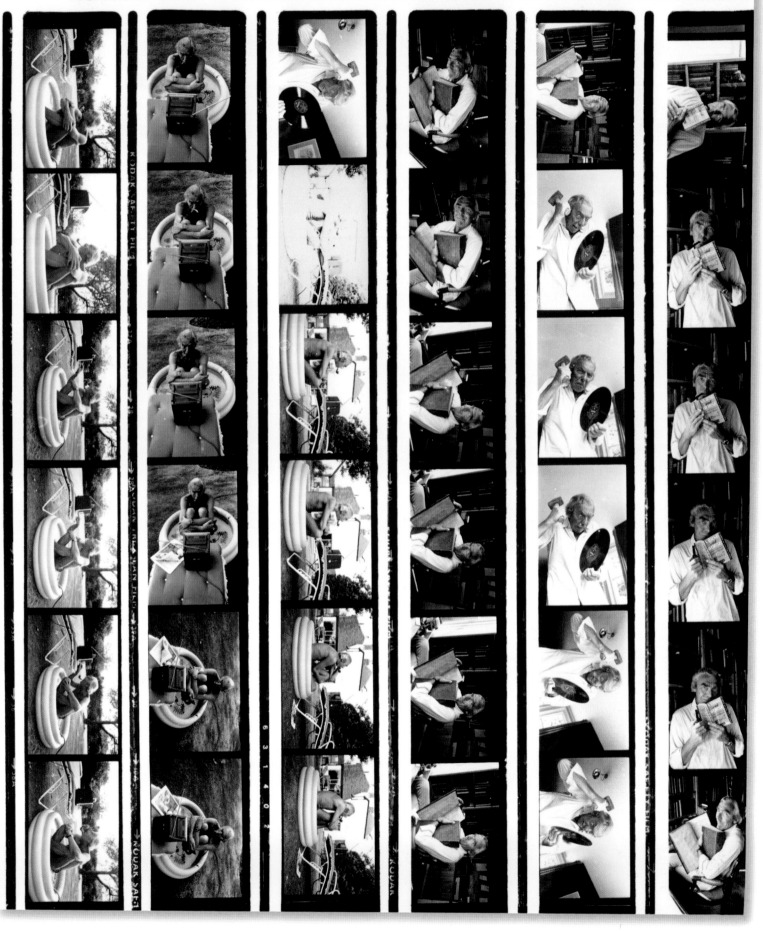

Frank Muir *Photographs by Jeremy Grayson* 1975

Warren Mitchell *Photograph by Jeremy Grayson 1973*

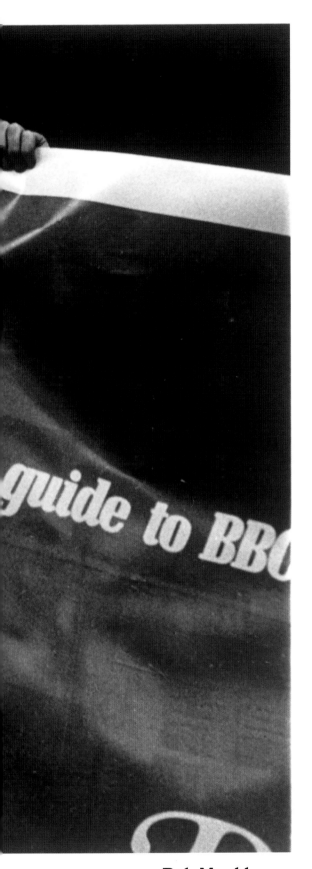

Bob Monkhouse
Photograph by Chris Ridley 1984

John Bird
Photograph by Don Smith

Sandi Toksvig
Photograph by
Sylvaine Poitau 2003

Joanna Lumley,
Dawn French &
Jennifer Saunders
Photographer unknown

Stephen Fry & Hugh Laurie
Photographer unknown

Griff Rhys Jones
Photograph by Mark Harrison

Paul Merton
Photograph by
Nicky Johnston 2003

Eric Sykes
*Photograph by
Jason Bell 2001*

Bobby Davro *Photograph by John Rogers* 1992

Graham Norton
Photograph by
Melanie Dunea
2001

PHOTOGRAPH BY DON SMITH

THAT WAS THE WEEK THAT W...

**Barry Cryer,
Graeme Garden,
Humphrey Lyttelton,
Tim Brooke-Taylor
& Tony Hawks**
*Photographed at a
recording of I'm Sorry
I Haven't a Clue at
the Wolverhampton
Grand Theatre
by Tom Howard 2001*

**David Frost, Willie Rushton,
Roy Kinnear, Millicent Martin,
Kenneth Cope, Lance Percival
& David Kernan**
*Photographed on the set of
That Was the Week That Was
by Don Smith 1963*

Alexei Sayle *Photograph by Bill Robinson*

Willie Rushton
Photograph by Don Smith 1970

Ricky Gervais *Photograph by Fergus Greer 2005*

**Matt Lucas,
Ricky Gervais
& David Walliams**
Photograph by Andy Earl 2003

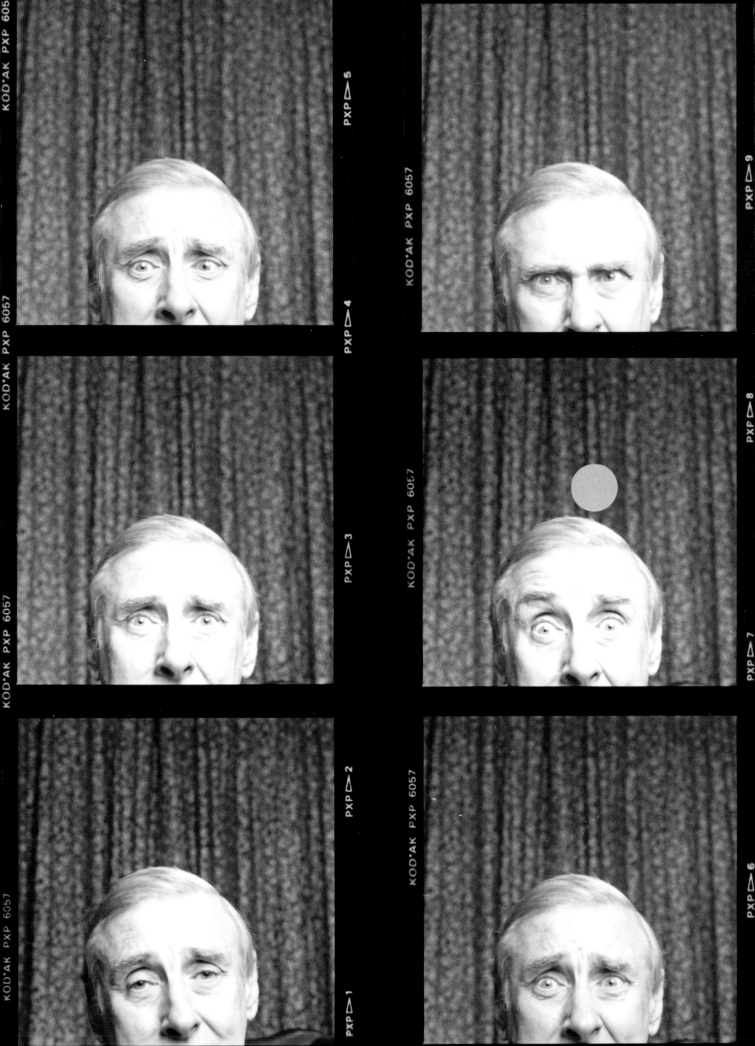

KOD·AK PXP 6057   KOD·AK PXP 605   PXP ▷ 5

KOD·AK PXP 6057   PXP ▷ 4   KOD·AK PXP 6057   PXP ▷ 9

KOD·AK PXP 6057   PXP ▷ 3   KOD·AK PXP 6057   PXF ▷ 8

KOD·AK PXP 6057   PXP ▷ 2   KOD·AK PXP 6057   PXF ▷ 7

PXP ▷ 1   KOD·AK PXP 6057   PXF ▷ 6

Sanjeev Bhaskar & Meera Syal *Photograph by Trevor Ray Hart*

Frank Thornton, Emma Thompson, Robert Lindsay, Bill Owen, Brian Wilde & Peter Sallis
Photographed for the Royal Variety Performance 1984

Alan Davies
Photograph by
Jonathan Glynn-Smith
2000

Derek Nimmo with Zee, Babs & Jackie *Photograph by Don Smith* 1974

Peter Cook & Dudley Moore
*Photographed on the set
of Not Only... But Also
by Don Smith*

**Jimmy Edwards,
Cyril Fletcher,
Tommy Trinder,
Ted Ray &
the head of
McDonald Hobley**
*Photographed on
the set of Does the
Team Think? by
Don Smith* 1958

Spike Milligan *Photograph by Don Smith* 1972

Johnny Vegas *Photograph by Tom Howard 2005*

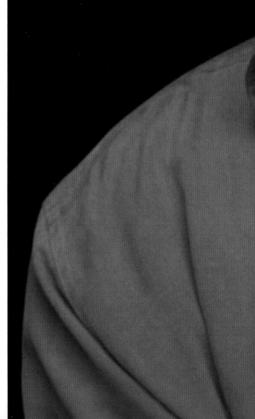

Lenny Henry
*Photograph by
Trevor Leighton*
2002

**Ernie Wise, Eric Morecambe
& Des O'Connor**
*Photographed during rehearsals
for The Morecambe and
Wise Christmas Show
by Don Smith* 1975

Prunella Scales
Photograph by Bill Robinson

Actresses

Lesley-Anne Down *Photograph by Tim Roney* 1980

Pauline Collins
Photograph by Sven Arnstein

Penelope Keith *Photograph by John Timbers* 1979

Julie Walters
Photograph by
Mark Harrison 2002

Geraldine McEwan
Photograph by Crispian Woodgate

Julie Walters
Photograph by
Jason Bell 2003

Joely Richardson *Photographer unknown*

Claire Goose
Photograph by
Barry J Holmes 1999

Vanessa Redgrave *Photograph by Jillian Edelstein 2005*

Shirley MacLaine
Photograph by Alan Strutt
2000

Samantha Bond
Photograph by Alistair Morrison

Beryl Reid
Photograph by Don Smith
1969

Kathleen Turner
Photograph by Caroline Mardon
1992

Ruby Wax, David Gest and Liza Minnelli
Photographed at the Sea Shell fish shop in London's Marylebone by James Stenson 2003

Brenda Blethyn *Photograph by Paul Rider*

Dervla Kirwan
Photograph by
Barry J Holmes 1999

Fenella Fielding
Photographs by
Don Smith 1963

Margaret Rutherford
Photographed at her home in
Gerrards Cross, Buckinghamshire
by Tony Ray-Jones 1970

Kate Winslet *Photograph by Jason Bell 2004*

Helen Mirren
Photograph by
Jason Bell 2003

Glenda Jackson *Photograph by Steve Bicknell* 1989

Olivia Newton-John
Photographer unknown
1977

Edith Evans
*Photograph by
Angus McBean*
1959

Joan Crawford
*Photograph by
Don Smith*
1956

Gillian Taylforth
*Photograph by
Mark Harrison*
1998

Judi Dench with Geoffrey Palmer
Photographed on the set of As Time Goes By for the last ever episode by Jason Bell 2002

Judi Dench *Photograph by Don Smith* 1985

**Judi Dench
with husband
Michael Williams**
*Photograph by
Chris Steele-Perkins*
1979

93

Cherie Lunghi
Photograph by
Rolph Gobits
1980

Emma Thompson
Photograph by
Brian Moody 1988

The audience of *Juke Box Jury*
Photograph by Don Smith 1961

Sammy Davis Jr
*Photographed at
BBC Television Centre
by Don Smith 1963*

98

Tom Jones *Photograph by Jason Bell 2003*

Oasis: Andy Bell, Liam Gallagher, Noel Gallagher & Gem Archer
Photograph by Andy Earl 2008

DAVID ESSEX *Photographer unknown* 1965

David Essex
*Photograph by
Les Wilson* 1997

Eric Clapton *Photograph by Terry O'Neill* 1990

Elton John *Photographs by James Dimmock 2002*

Cilla Black
Photographer unknown

Shirley Bassey
Photograph by Richard Farley

Lynsey de Paul
*Photograph by
Don Smith* 1973

John Peel *Photograph by Fergus Greer 2001*

John Peel
Photograph by Chris Ridley

Jools Holland
*Photographed on the set of Later...
with Jools Holland
by Mark Harrison
2004*

Leonard Bernstein
Photograph by
Robin Laurance 1975

Aled Jones
*Photograph
by Clive Barda*
1985

**Michael Parkinson
& Nigel Kennedy**
*Photographs by
Tim Roney* 1985

113

Mrs Mills & Reg Dixon *Photographer unknown* 1971

Ian Dury *Photograph by Chris Ridley 1982*

Kenny Everett
Photographs by
Don Smith 1967

Bob Harris
Photograph by
Colin Bell 2001

Noel Edmonds *Photographer unknown* 1982

Mike Reid & John Craven
Photographer unknown

Tony Blackburn
Photograph by Richard Farley 1974

Peter Powell *Photographer unknown*

Rick Wakeman
*Photograph by
Terry Fincher* 1975

Johnnie Walker
*Photograph by
Don Smith* 1975

Pan's People *Photograph by Don Smith* 1973

Robert Plant *Photograph by Colin Bell 2005*

Suzi Quatro *Photograph by Gemma Day 2006*

Millicent Martin with Lance Percival & Al Mancini
*Photographed on the set of That Was the Week That Was
by Don Smith 1963*

John Denver
Photograph by Don Smith 1973

**U2: The Edge, Adam Clayton,
Bono & Larry Mullen Jr**
Photograph by Mark Allan 2005

Evelyn Glennie
Photograph by Alan Strutt 2000

Val Doonican
*Photographed on the set of his BBC TV show
by Don Smith 1960s*

Val Doonican's rocking chair
Photograph by Tim Roney

Anthony Hopkins
Photograph by Nigel Parry 1993

David Niven *Photographer unknown*

David Suchet
Photograph by Jason Bell 2001

Ian McKellen
*Photographer
unknown 1972*

Leo McKern
*Photographed during
a read-through of
Our Mutual Friend
by Don Smith* 1976

Dennis Waterman
*Photographed in the home
dressing room of Chelsea FC
by Mark Harrison 2003*

Sean Bean
Photograph by Nigel Parry 1993

EPP ▶ 8

Oliver Reed
*Photographs
by Caroline
Mardon*

John Simm
Photograph by Mark Harrison 2000

David Tennant
Photograph by Ellis Parrinder 2005

Jon Pertwee
Photograph by David Magnus
1970

Peter O'Toole
*Photograph by
Don Smith* 1972

Ian McShane
Photographs by Jillian Edelstein 2004

Robert Vaughn
Photograph by Jason Bell 2004

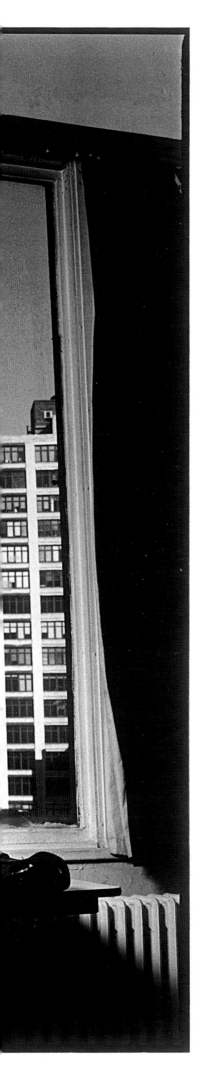

Richard Briers *Photograph by Nigel Parry* 1993

Anthony Hopkins
Photograph by Nigel Parry 1993

Martin Clunes
Photographs by Jillian Edelstein 2005

Jonny Lee Miller
Photograph by John Stoddart 2003

148

Denis Lawson
*Photograph by
Steve Shipman*

Brian Capron & Leslie Grantham
Photograph by Trevor Ray Hart 2003

MATCH COVER TO ABOVE RESULT
CONTRAST WISE.

James Nesbitt
Photograph by
Barry J Holmes 2001

Derek Jacobi
Photograph by
Dan Goldsmith 2004

John Hurt *Photograph by Sven Arnstein 2003*

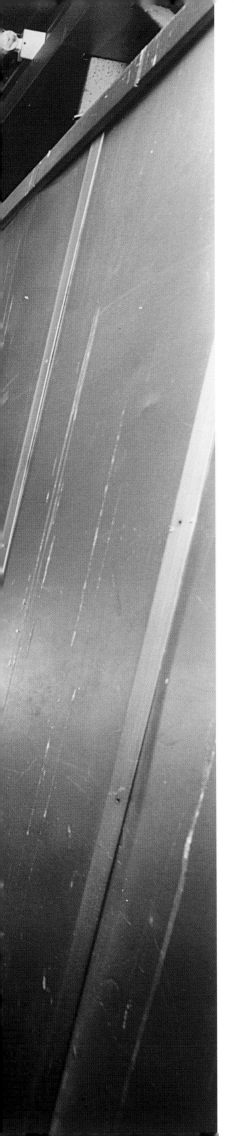

Bill Nighy *Photograph by Mark Harrison 2003*

Kenneth Branagh
Photograph by Jason Bell 2002

155

DONALD PLEASENCE (taken 23.5.62)

Pics - Don Smith

Donald Pleasence
Photographs by
Don Smith 1962

Bob Hoskins
Photograph by
Nigel Parry 1993

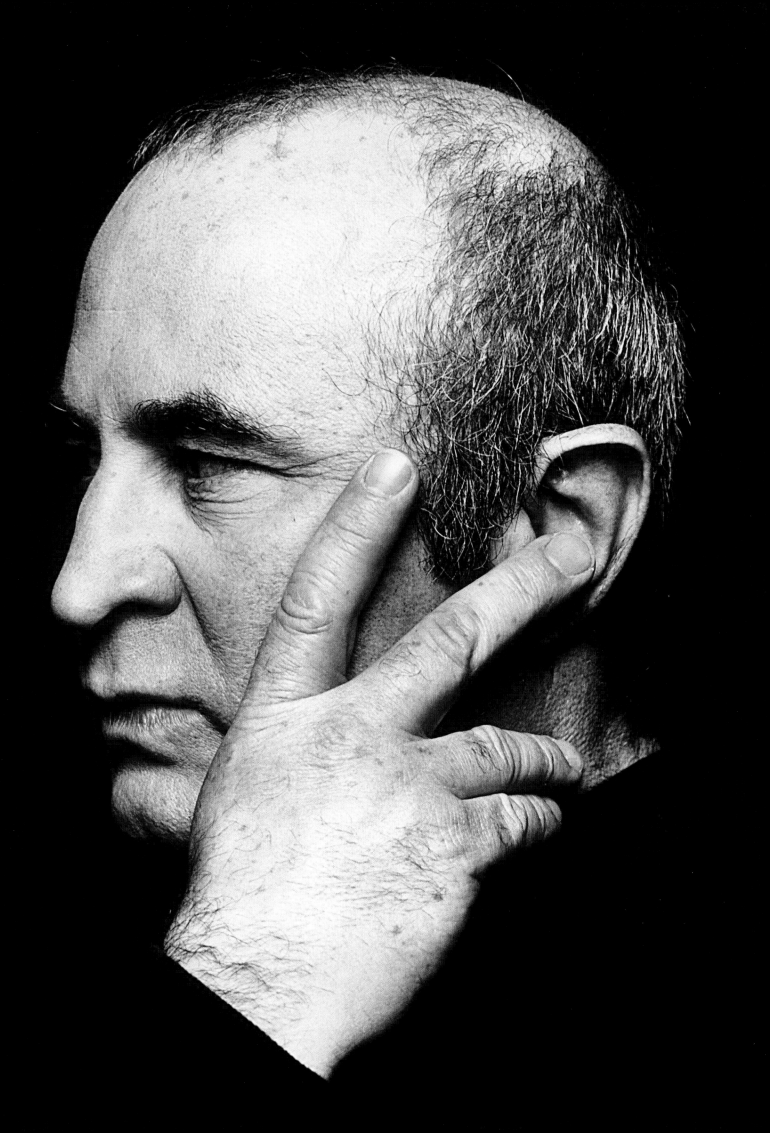

Rufus Sewell
Photograph by Andy Earl 2003

Mark Strong
Photograph by Julian Dodd 2005

Jack Davenport
Photograph by
Nicky Johnston 1997

Nicholas Lyndhurst *Photograph by Mark Harrison*

Albert Finney
Photograph by
Nicky Johnston 2001

Colin Firth *Photographer unknown*

TRUNK CURL
BURPEE JUMP
DERSAL RISE
TUCK JUMP
PRESS UP CLAP
SQUAT JUMP
SIT UPS
PIKE JUMP

Ray Winstone
Photograph by
Neil Cooper 2002

Ross Kemp
*Photograph by
Mike Owen* 1998

David Jason *Photograph by Nigel Parry* 1993

Alan Bates *Photograph by Nigel Parry* 1992

John Nettles *Photograph by Chris Ridley* 1990

Damian Lewis
*Photographed for
the Stephen
Poliakoff drama
Friends and
Crocodiles by
Jude Edginton
2005*

Tony Robinson
Photograph by
Bill Robinson 1993

Leslie Phillips *Photograph by Jason Bell 2000*

Jeremy Paxman *Photograph by Mark Harrison* 1997

**Jonathan Ross,
Terry Wogan &
John Humphrys**
*Photograph by
Michael Birt* 2005

Rachel de Thame *Photograph by Mike Owen* 2001

That's Life **presenters**
Esther Rantzen, Adrian Mills,
Grant Baynham & Gavin Campbell
Photograph by Clive Arrowsmith 1988

Magnus Magnusson
Photographer unknown 1972

Jonathan Ross
Photograph by Steve Pyke 1987

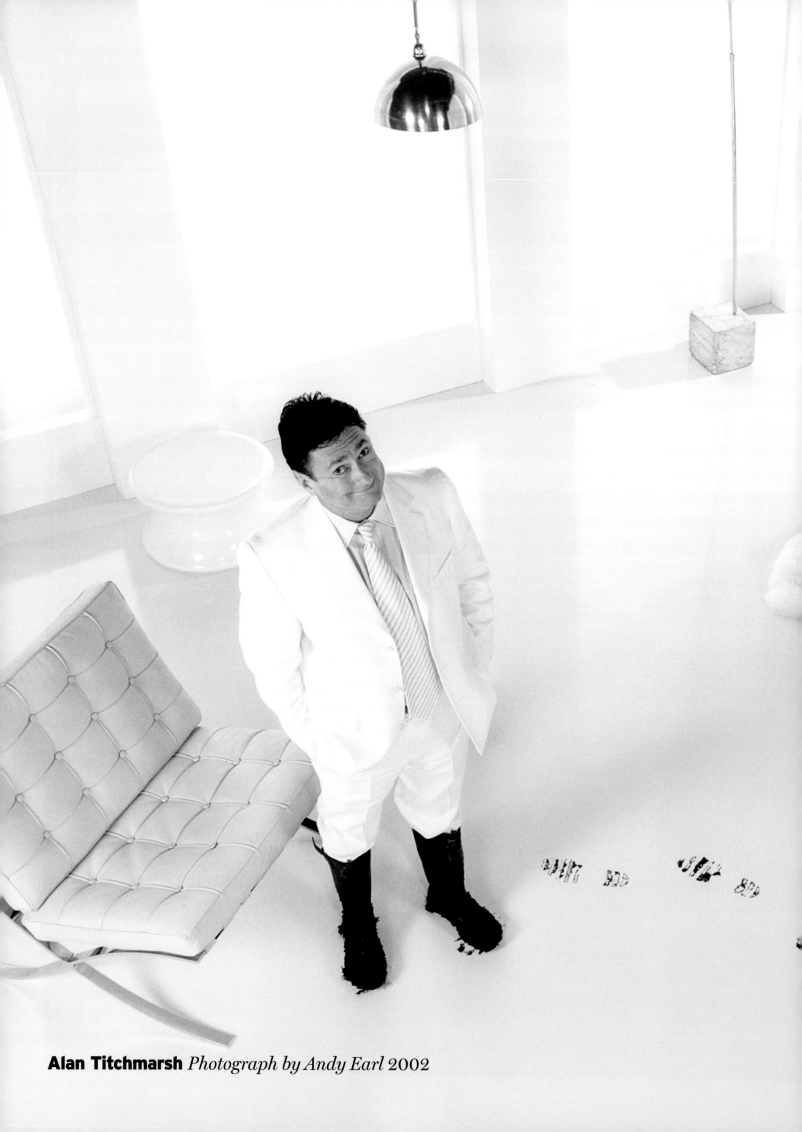

Alan Titchmarsh *Photograph by Andy Earl 2002*

Johnny Morris *Photographer unknown*

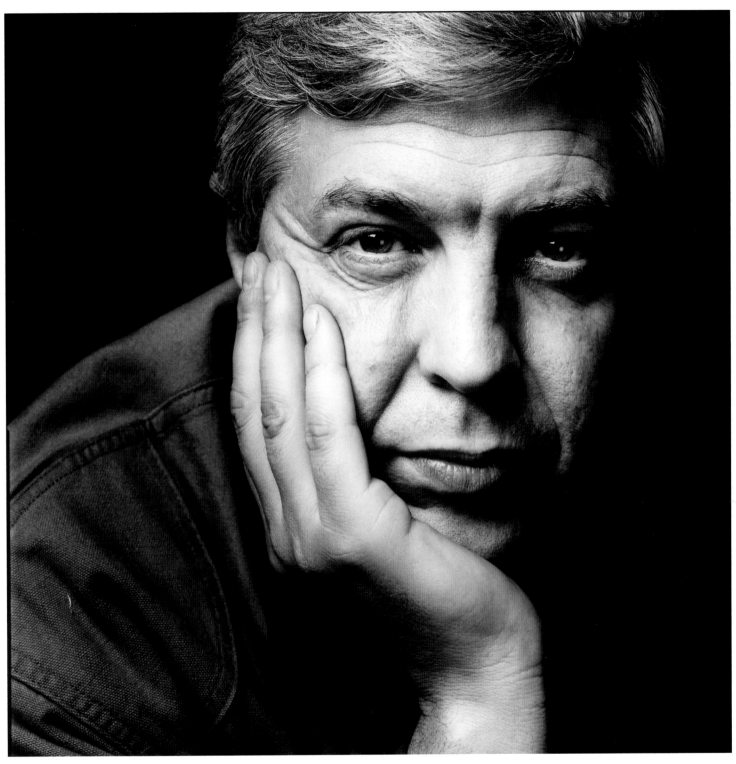

John Simpson *Photograph by Nigel Parry* 1991

FUJI RDP

CABCAC-ACIG

RDP ▷ 2

Jeremy Clarkson
Photographer unknown

David Dimbleby
Photograph by
Chris Steele-Perkins
1979

Cliff Michelmore
Photographed with
the studio set model
for the BBC's
General Election
programme by
Martin Breese 1970

**Jonathan Dimbleby &
his then wife Bel Mooney**
*Photograph by
Don Smith* 1971

Sue MacGregor
Photographer unknown 1986

Kate Humble
*Photographs by
Jonathan Glynn-Smith
2000*

188

Ulrika Jonsson *Photographer unknown*

Chris Evans
Photograph by
Mark Harrison
1992

BBC weathermen, clockwise from top left: Richard Angwin, Michael Fish, Ian McCaskill & Bill Giles *Photographer unknown* 1984

Bill Oddie
Photographed in the garden of his London home by Andy Earl 2003

Keith Chegwin
Photographer unknown

Michael Parkinson
Photographer unknown

TISWAS presenters
Chris Tarrant & Sally James
Photograph by David Venni

Tomorrow's World presenters
Raymond Baxter & Judith Hann
Photographer unknown

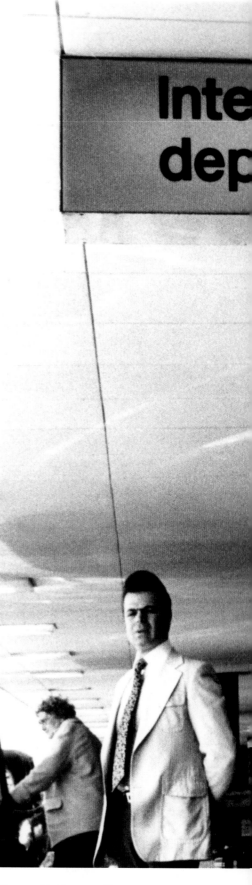

Rageh Omaar
Photograph by
Ellis Parrinder 2003

Joan Bakewell
Photograph by
Don Smith 1979

Kirsty Wark
Photographer unknown

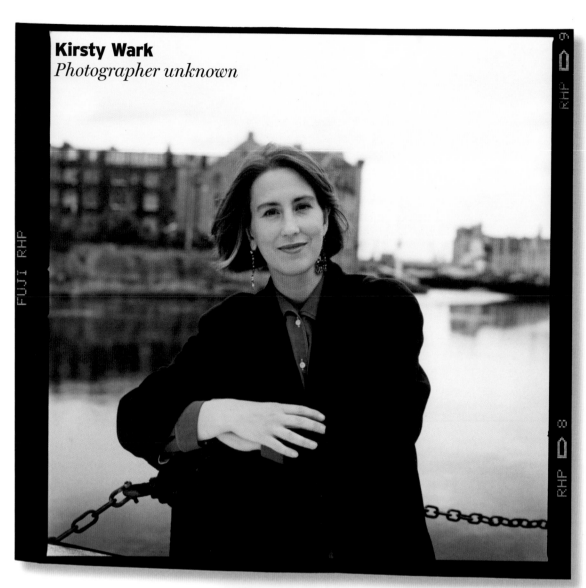

Orla Guerin
*Photograph by
David Silverman
2003*

Jeremy Paxman
Photograph by Terry O'Neill 1990

Hugh Scully & *Antiques Roadshow* experts
Photographer unknown

John Craven
Photographer unknown 1972

Fred Dibnah
Photographed with his first wife Alison by David Chadwick

Charlotte Green & Terry Wogan
Photograph by Mark Harrison 2002

Stephen Fry
Photograph by
Jillian Edelstein 2005

David Attenborough *Photograph by Jeremy Grayson* 1974

David Attenborough *Photograph by Andy Earl* 2003

**John &
Simon King**
*Photograph by
Clive Landen* 1984

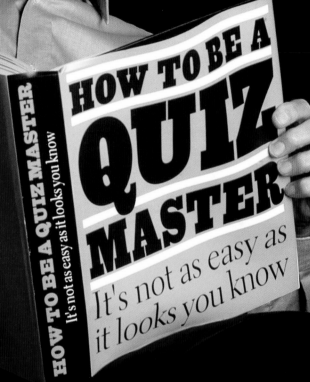

Andrew Marr *Photograph by Jason Bell 2001*

John Humphrys
*Photographed for his debut as questionmaster
on Mastermind by Nicky Johnston 2003*

Graham Norton
*Photograph by
James Stenson 2005*

Ant & Dec – Anthony McPartlin and Declan Donnelly
Photograph by Nicky Johnston 1996

Peter Purves, Valerie Singleton, John Noakes with Petra, Jason and Shep
Photograph by Penny Tweedie 1971

Blue Peter badge
Photographer unknown

Lesley Judd
*Photograph by
John Timbers
1977*

Robin Day
Photographs by
Chris Ridley 1984

John Sergeant *Photograph by Jason Bell* 2001

Louis Theroux *Photograph by Jason Bell*

Laurence Llewelyn-Bowen
Photograph by Nicky Johnston

Alan Titchmarsh
Photograph by Barry J Holmes 2001

Sue Lawley
Photographer unknown

Peter Sissons
Photographer unknown

222

Michael Palin
Photograph by Mark Harrison 2004

Bruce Forsyth
*Photographed at the
London Palladium
for his 80th birthday
by Joel Anderson 2008*

Jeremy Clarkson
Photograph by Barry J Holmes 1998

Barry Norman
Photographer unknown

Simon Hoggart
Photograph by Chris Ridley 1981

Derek Jameson
Photographer unknown

Mariella Frostrup
Photographs by Jillian Edelstein 2004

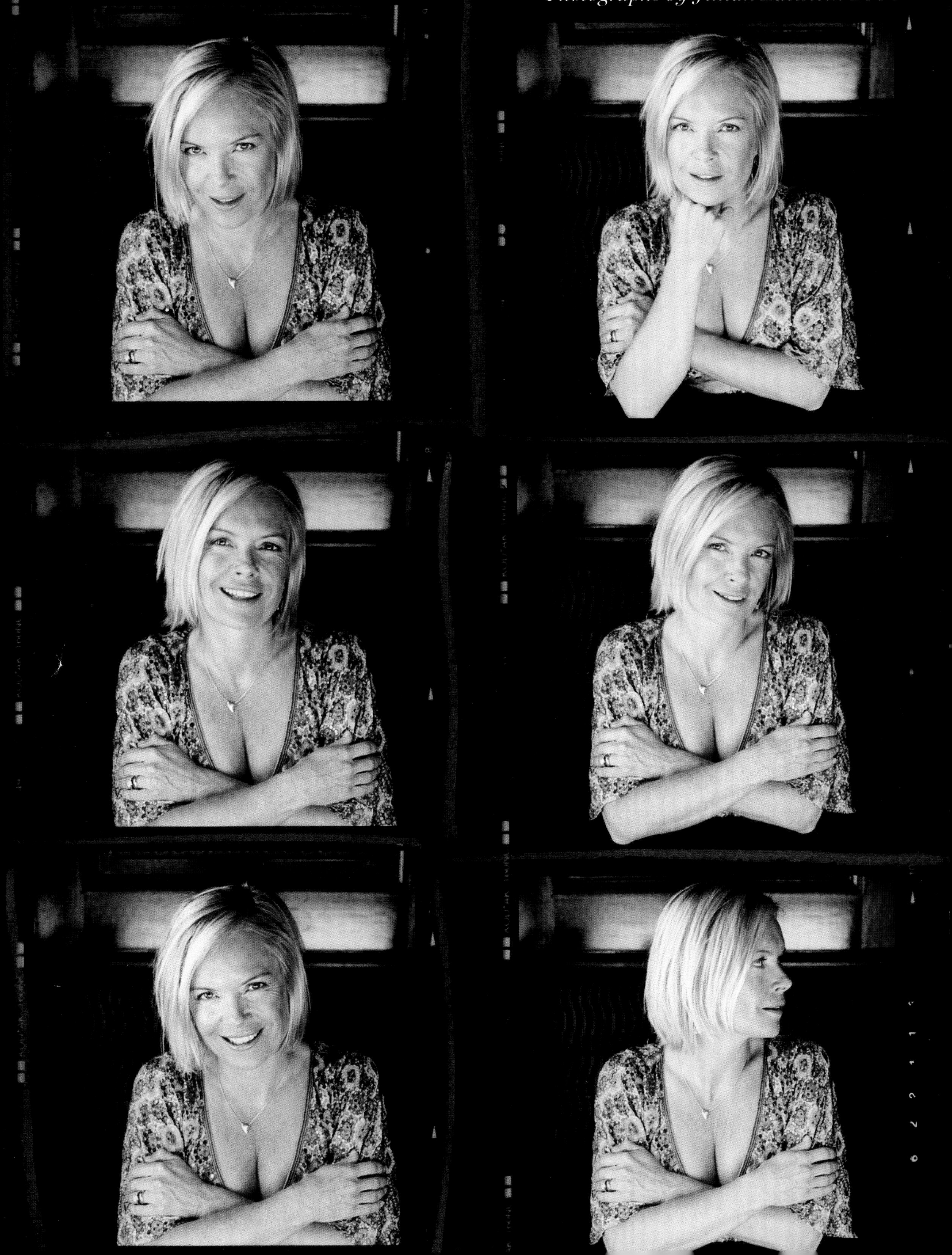

Tony Hart & Morph *Photograph by Don Smith* 1980

Terry Nation
*Photographed for
a Radio Times
Dalek competition
by Don Smith* 1972

Basil Brush
Photograph by Don Smith

Richard Dimbleby
Photographed on the set of Panorama by Don Smith 1961

David Attenborough
Photograph by
Nadav Kander 2012

David Beckham & Alan Hansen
Photograph by Mike Owen 1999

SPORT

MOTD

BIRD
John

TIME
CAPSULE

TIME
CAPSULE

The
Time of
my life

E G

FEATURES ©

Jayne Torvill & Christopher Dean
Photographer unknown

Desmond Lynam
Photographer unknown 1982

Daley Thompson *Photographer unknown* 1989

Paula Radcliffe
*Photographed at her training
camp in the French Pyrenees
by Andy Earl* 2004

Dick Emery & Graham Hill
*Photographed for Dick Emery's Grand Prix at
Snetterton in Norfolk by Philip Sayer 1970*

Kevin Keegan *Photograph by Allan Ballard* 1974

Peter Shilton *Photograph by Terry O'Neill* 1990

Lennox Lewis *Photograph by Nigel Parry 2001*

Desmond Lynam
Photograph by
Jillian Edelstein 2004

Peter O'Sullevan
*Photographed at Aintree with his crib sheet of runners
for the Grand National by Bob Martin* 1990

Murray Walker
Photograph by Mark Harrison

Bill McLaren *Photograph by Keith McMillan* 1977

**John Arlott &
Brian Johnston**
Photographer unknown

Morgan *Photographs by Don Smith* 1969

Alan Hansen & Jimmy Hill
Scotland and England were drawn in the same group for Euro 96.
Photograph by Ian McKinnell 1996

Alex Ferguson
Pictured at Old Trafford, photographer unknown

Boris Becker *Photograph by Jason Bell* 2001

Tim Foster, Matthew Pinsent, James Cracknell & Steve Redgrave *Photograph by Jason Bell*

Steve Redgrave *Photograph by Andy Earl*

David Vine
*Photograph by
Colin Rowe* 1968

Karen Pickering
*Photograph by
Bill Robinson*

Jimmy Hill
Photographed in the Coventry City home dressing room by Barry Wilkinson 1976

Stanley Matthews
Photographed (top) for his 50th birthday and impending knighthood by Don Smith 1965

Vinnie Jones
Photographs (right) by Jonathan Glynn-Smith 2000

Ian Poulter, Graeme McDowell & Nick Dougherty
Photograph by Hugo Dixon 2003

Ronnie O'Sullivan
*Photograph by
Nicky Johnston
2001*

Delia Smith & Jamie Oliver *Photograph by Andy Earl 2003*

Michael Heseltine
Photograph by Mark Harrison 2000

Tony Benn
Photograph by Nigel Parry 1993

Alan Bennett
Photographer unknown

Roger McGough
Photographed on the Birkenhead Ferry,
Merseyside, by Warwick Bedford 1981

VS Naipaul *Photographer unknown*

John Betjeman *Photograph by Don Smith*

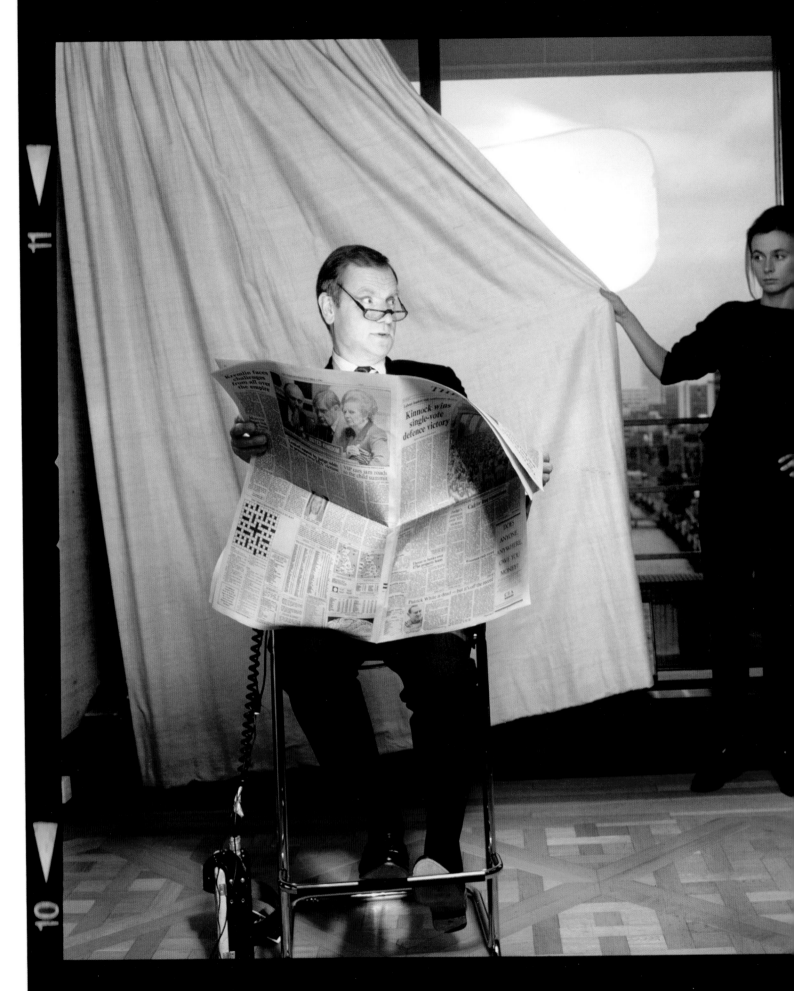

AGFA 100 RS

1810

Piers Morgan *Photograph by John Swannell* 2003

Jeffrey Archer
Photograph by Chris Ridley 1990

Feliks Topolski
The painter in his studio at work on a 100ft mural, commissioned by Prince Philip, showing the Queen's coronation. Photographer unknown 1960

George Bernard Shaw *Photographer unknown*

WH Auden *Photographed during the poet's appearance on Parkinson by David Edwards* 1972

Sue Townsend
Photograph by
Mike Putland 1983

John le Carré & James Naughtie
Photographed at le Carré's house in Cornwall by Gary Moyes 2003

Delia Smith & husband Michael Wynn-Jones
Photograph by Norman Hollands 1975

Gary Rhodes
Photograph by
Scarlet Page

Gordon Ramsay
& Angela Hartnett
Photograph by
Richard Ansett

Barnes Wallis *Photograph by Jeremy Grayson 1974*

PL Travers
*Photograph by
Clive Barda 1977*

Kenneth Tynan *Photograph by Roger Mayne*

Gordon Ramsay
Photograph by
Mark Harrison 2004

Nigella Lawson *Photograph by Andy Earl 2001*

**Ernie Wise
& Eric Morecambe**
Photograph by Don Smith
1976